Make a Cloud, Measure the Wind

Contents

Written by Luther Reimer

What Will the Weather Be Like?

Weather is all around us and it can change day by day. If you know what the weather is going to be like, you can plan what you are going to do to fit in with the weather. You can wear the right clothes so you won't get wet if it rains, or too hot if it is sunny.

Make a Cloud

No matter what type of day it is there are often clouds in the sky. Some clouds are fluffy, some clouds are wispy, some clouds are dark, and some clouds are light. Different types of clouds tell us what the weather might be like.

What You Will Need to Make a Cloud

- a container with a metal lid
- some ice cubes
- some very warm water

What to Do

Follow the arrows and watch what happens.

Step 1

Put some warm water into the container.

Step 2

Place the lid upside down on the container.

Step 3

Put the ice cubes on top of the lid.

Make a Wind Direction Recorder

A wind direction recorder shows the direction the wind is coming from. You can use a wind direction recorder over a number of days to build up a picture of wind patterns for the place where you live.

What You Will Need to Make a Wind Direction Recorder

- a drinking straw
- a small compass
- an empty plastic pot with a lid
- some sand and stones to fill the pots
- a 6 inch (15 cm) pencil with an eraser on its end
- a long pin
- a waterproof marker pen
- a stapler
- some thick plastic you can cut with scissors
- scissors

What to Do

Follow the arrows below to make your own wind direction recorder.

Step 1

Mark out an arrowhead shape on the plastic sheet and use the scissors to cut it out. Make an arrow tail shape the same way.

Step 2

Staple the arrowhead and arrow tail onto the straw so it looks like this.

Next Page

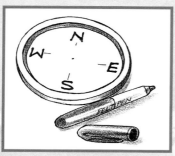

Step 3

Use the marker pen to make the pot lid into a compass with marks in the right places for North (N), South (S), East (E) and West (W).

Step 4

Make a hole in the middle of the lid just big enough for the pencil to fit in.

Step 5

Fill the pot with some heavy stones in the bottom and cover them with sand. Fill the pot right up.

Step 6
Push the pencil through the hole in the lid so the eraser end is at the top.

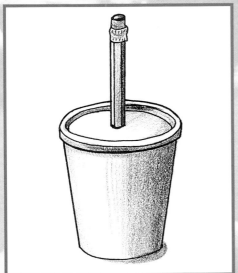

Step 7
Push the lead end of the pencil into the pot and put the lid on the pot. Make sure the pencil stands up straight.

Next Page

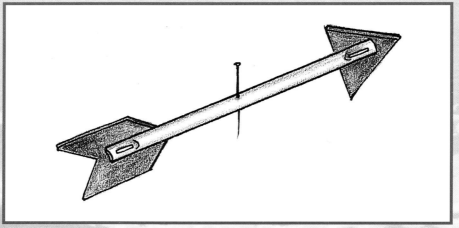

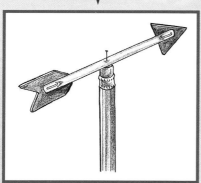

Step 8
Push the long pin right through the middle of the straw arrow.

Step 9
Push the end of the long pin into the eraser on the top of the pencil.

Next Page

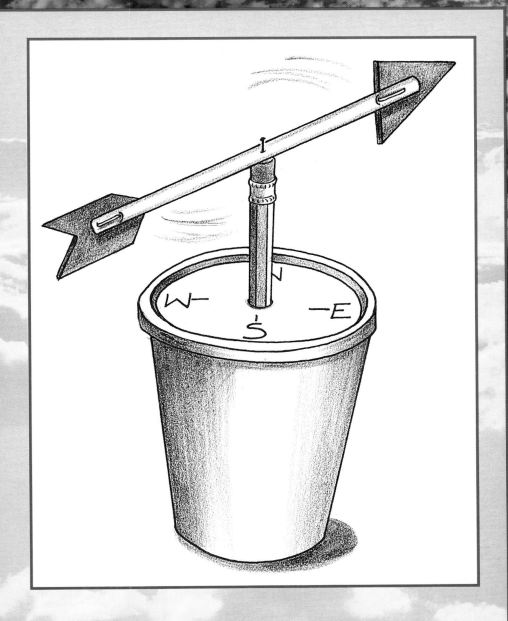

Your wind direction recorder should look like this.

Using Your Wind Direction Recorder

Take your wind direction recorder outside when the wind is blowing. Use the compass to find north. Hold the compass steady and turn it slowly until the needle of the compass is pointing to N (north).

Put your wind direction recorder on the ground. Turn it so the N on its lid points to the same place as the N on the compass in your hand.

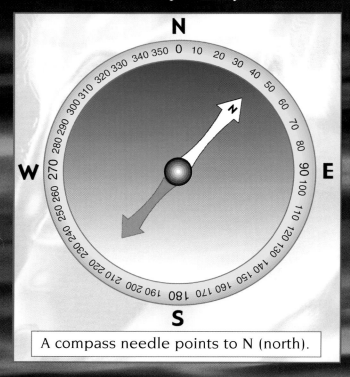

A compass needle points to N (north).

The wind will blow your wind direction recorder around. Watch as the arrow turns around. See which way it is pointing by looking at the directions you marked on the lid.

Which compass point is the arrow pointing to?

If it is pointing between two different points, which one is it pointing closest to? This is the name of the direction the wind is blowing from.

Wind Directions

A north wind blows from the north. It blows to the south. An east wind blows from the east. It blows to the west.

Keeping Wind Direction Records

By taking a measurement each day at the same time you can build up a record of the wind direction for where you live.

Monday

The wind direction was north.

Tuesday

The wind direction today was from the north.

Wednesday

The wind direction today was northeast.

Thursday

The wind direction was northeast.

Friday

The wind direction was from the east.

This will show which direction the wind blows from most often for your area. This wind has a special name. This wind is called the prevailing wind.

Wind Direction Results	
Day	Wind Direction
Monday	north
Tuesday	north
Wednesday	northeast
Thursday	northeast
Friday	east

Index